This book belongs to:

.....Alyssa Taitt..............

...................Love Grandma....

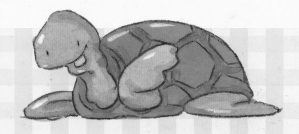

Written by Jillian Harker

Illustrated by Rachael O'Neill

This edition published by Parragon in 2010

Parragon
Queen Street House
4 Queen Street
Bath BA1 1HE, UK

ISBN 978-1-4454-1673-1

Printed in China

Let's Share!

PaRRagon
Bath · New York · Singapore · Hong Kong · Cologne · Delhi · Melbourne

Mind your child's manners!

It's important to start teaching good manners early so they become a habit for life. The stories in the MIND YOUR MANNERS! series are written to make learning good manners a positive experience.

Here are some of the ways you can help to make it fun:

* Find a quiet time to look at this story together and encourage your child to join in. The rhymes make the story easy to remember.

* After every question, talk about what you might say or do. Ask your child for suggestions. Joining in will help them to learn.

* Use the pages at the end of the story to check that your child understands when it is appropriate to use good manners.

* Throughout the day, reward your child's good manners with plenty of praise.

"That looks fun!
Can I play, too,
And share your
bouncy ball with you?"

"I will share my ball with you.

"Playing ball's more fun with two!"

"That looks fun!
Can I paddle, too,
And share your cool
tide pool with you?"

"I'll share my pool with you.

"Paddling is more fun with two!"

"That looks fun!
Can I dig, too,
And share your
shovel and pail with you?"

"I'll share my shovel and pail with you,

"Digging is more fun with two!"

"That looks good!
Can we share, too,
And eat your picnic
snack with you?"

"No!
I don't want to share my
picnic with you!"

How rude!

"Oops! Sorry, I forgot,

"You've all shared with me a lot.

"I would love to share with you,

"Sharing's much more fun to do!"

What will you do?

When someone asks to join your game, what will you do?

If you said "Let's share," you were right!

When someone asks to share your special place, what will you do?

If you said "Let's share," you were right!

 When someone asks to play
with your toy, what will you do?

If you said "Let's share," you were right!

 When someone asks to share
your food, what will you do?

If you said "Let's share," you were right!

Did you say "Let's share" in all
the right places?